THE AUDITION GUIDE

Acknowledgments

I would like to thank the following people for making this book possible:

My mother and father, Linda Hurst, Mauro Vigliotti and Alvaro Quinteros. My brothers, Gonzalo and Ramiro, and my sisters, Romina and Julieta.

Contents

Ear Training

Sight Reading

Improvisation

The Interview

Preparation & Tips

About the Author

Preface

This guide is the result of years of formal music training. It has been crafted by combining my formal studies, my preparation for the audition and my audition experience, with all the comments and questions about the audition that I received on YouTube and the audition guidelines from *www.berklee.edu*.

This book is meant to guide the reader as they prepare for a guitar audition at Berklee College of Music. Instead of reading this guide in one sitting, the applicant should use the book throughout their entire preparation.

This book will help you prepare for the Audition and Interview process. I will describe every aspect of the process that will contribute to your acceptance to Berklee College of Music. I will talk about all the music concepts you need to learn before going to your audition; I will recommend you books, software, websites and more. I will show you how to manage your study time without leaving anything behind. I will share my experience about the audition and interview. I will tell you everything you need to know about the audition and interview process.

CHAPTER I

BERKLEE
COLLEGE OF MUSIC

BERKLEE

Berklee College of Music is the world's largest and most diverse music college. Founded in 1945, it has become a school where thousands of musicians from all over the world want to go to pursue a music career. With more than 4,000 students, the college focuses on different music genres like Jazz, Rock, R&B, Country, Funk, Film Scoring and Classical Music. With students coming from 96 countries, a faculty made up of 564 members, and more than 250 Grammy awards collectively won by alumni, Berklee is becoming the world's leading institute of contemporary music.

PRINCIPAL INSTRUMENT

All students must declare a principal instrument. They can choose from 29 different instruments: Banjo, Baritone Horn, Acoustic Bass, Electric Bass, Bassoon, Cello, Clarinet, Drum Set, Flute, French Horn, Guitar, Harp, Mandolin, Marimba, Oboe, Percussion, Hand Percussion, Acoustic Piano, Alto Saxophone, Baritone Saxophone, Tenor Saxophone, Trombone, Bass Trombone, Trumpet, Tuba, Vibraphone, Viola, Violin and Voice.

Major

You can choose between two programs: Degree or Diploma. A Degree combines music studies with liberal arts courses, while a Diploma is only focused on music. The school offers Degree or Diploma in 12 majors: Composition, Contemporary Writing and Production, Film Scoring, Jazz Composition, Music Business/Management, Music Education, Music Production and Engineering, Electronic Production and Design, Music Therapy, Performance, Professional Music and Songwriting. You can declare one major or, depending on the program, two majors.

Campus

Berklee College of Music campus is made up of 22 buildings, offering approximately 300 practice rooms where students can get together to jam, practice with their band, work on their principal instrument and more. It has 63 rooms specially designed for Ensemble playing, 13 fully equipped recording studios, 6 film/video scoring labs, 9 electronic production and design rooms and 5 performance venues offering more than a thousand concerts annually. The school also has 275 acoustic pianos, 5 radio channels and 250 computer-based music workstations.

For more information visit *www.berklee.edu*

How to apply

If you want to study at Berklee College of Music you must first apply. Some international students are used to signing up for college and immediately getting a seat for the upcoming academic year; but in the United States, and especially in private institutions, signing up for college is a whole different thing. To be accepted as a student at Berklee College of Music you must first:

- *Complete an application form provided by Berklee College of Music at www.berklee.edu*

- Send a legal and official translated copy of your high school diploma.

- If you are an international student or have studied outside of U.S, you will need to submit your transcripts by an accredited credential evaluation agency, such as Education Credential Evaluators *www.ece.org*

- If you graduated from college, you must send a legal and official translated copy of your diploma.

- If you are a Transfer Student, you must also send a legal and official translated copy of your transcripts with all completed college-level work.

- Send at least three recommendation letters: one from a music instructor, one from an important person of your city (e.g. high school principal, teacher, politician) and if English is not your primary language, you must also send a letter of recommendation from an English instructor. But if English is your primary language, it will be a good idea to send another letter from a second music instructor.

- If English is not your primary language, you are required to submit a TOEFL or IELTS score with your application. A TOEFL score of 72 or higher is recommended. An IELTS score of 6 or higher is recommended.

- SAT/ACT scores are optional. If you decide to send them, you need a score of C+ or higher in English, Math, History and Science.

- *You must also participate in a live audition and interview.*

- You must pay a $150 non-refundable application fee.

Application Form

To apply for Berklee College of Music you have to:

1. Go to *www.berklee.edu*

2. Click on *Admissions*

3. Once you are there, click on *Apply*, located on the left side.

4. You will need to create an account. Click on *Register* and after that on *Undergraduate Admissions.*

5. Fill in the form with all your personal information.

6. The information entered at this stage is not final; you can alter it at any time later. This information is required to create an account at Berklee; it is not the actual application. Also, your choice of major is not final; in fact, you won't choose your major until your 3rd semester at Berklee. Also, remember that you can always call Berklee and they will be happy to help you change anything in your application.

7. Once you click *submit*, you will receive a confirmation email with your account details. You can now login to your account and start your application.

The rest of the application is very simple. You will have to fill out typical contact information about you and your parents like, complete name, address, phone number, email, country of citizenship and more. You will have to specify the semester and program (Degree or Diploma) you are applying for. You will also have to select your two audition site choices; I strongly recommend selecting Boston as one of the options and, if possible, as your main option, because you will have the opportunity to explore the campus and potentially meet with students. If traveling to Boston is not an option for you, Berklee offers a world scholarship tour every year, which takes place in different countries and cities. For a complete and up to date list of countries visit *www.berklee.edu*. Among many other things, you will have to choose your principal instrument and intended field of study (major). Your choice of major is not final until your third semester at Berklee. Always check your spelling and grammar with an instructor or with anybody who writes very well in English.

Berklee offers three semesters per academic year, which you can apply for: Fall, Summer and Spring.

Fall Semester — Early Action

Fall is the regular semester in which all courses are available and the one that almost everyone applies for. If you apply for Fall semester early action, you will have to complete the application and send all supporting material (high school records, college transcripts for transfer students, application fee, etc.) on or before November 1st. Auditions and interviews for Fall semester early action take place from August through December, and admission decisions are issued on January 31st. So if you decide to apply for Fall semester 2015 early action, you will have to complete the application and send the supporting material on or before November 1st of 2014, take an audition and interview from August through December 2014, receive an admission decision on January 31st, 2015 and if you get accepted, start college in September, 2015. You will be given an Audition date once you submit your application to Berklee College of Music.

Fall Semester - Regular Action

If you choose Fall semester regular action, you will have to complete the application and send all material on or before January 15th, take the audition and interview between August and March and get an admission decision on March 31st. Regular action applicants, if accepted, also start classes in September.

Summer Semester

For Summer semester you will have to complete the application and send everything on or before December 1st, take the audition and interview between August and January and receive an admission decision on March 1st. Summer applicants, if accepted, start college in May.

Spring Semester

For Spring semester you will have to complete the application and send the supporting material on or before July 1st, take an audition and interview between March and July and get an admission decision on September 15th. Spring applicants, if accepted, start college in January.

Submitting your application

In order to submit your application, you will have to pay a non-refundable 150 dollar fee. Once you have submitted your application you will have to wait to receive an invitation for an audition and interview. *The audition process is the most important part in your application to Berklee*, even more important than the online application.

Scholarship

The audition and interview are both part of the scholarship process. You don't have to audition again to apply for a scholarship; every applicant is automatically considered for one. You could get accepted and receive no scholarship, or you could get accepted and be awarded a 5,000 dollar scholarship per year, 10,000, 20,000, or you could even get in and be awarded a full scholarship! Whether or not you get a scholarship will be based on how well you do on your audition and interview. It is important for you to know that it is not a financial-based scholarship; the amount you are awarded is not related to your financial situation. The decision is based on your level of musicianship demonstrated during the audition and interview process.

If you cannot make it to the audition, don't worry, you can always defer your application to another semester or change the audition date. Just make sure to call Berklee and let them know ahead of time.

CHAPTER II

AUDITION & INTERVIEW

HOW IT WORKS

The Audition and Interview are the most important part of the application to Berklee College of Music; they are both required.

You will have fifteen minutes to warm up on your instrument and review the reading material before going into the audition room. The audition will be fifteen minutes long and will be divided in different sections where you will:

— Play a prepared piece of your choice.

— Demonstrate your lead sheet and chord reading abilities.

— Improvise over a simple-form blues, standard jazz tune or harmonic vamp.

— Participate in ear training exercises.

As I mentioned before, you will have to participate in a fifteen minute interview with a Berklee admissions representative to discuss your goals and to talk about why Berklee would accept you as part of their community. You will also have the opportunity to talk about your past achievements or anything you want to share with Berklee about yourself.

AUDITION TESTIMONIES

My Audition

I auditioned for Berklee College of Music on December 6, 2008 in Boston, MA, U.S. My audition was scheduled for 10A.M, so I woke up at 7A.M and went to the 921 Boylston Street building at around 9 A.M. There was a huge sign at the entrance saying "Auditions & Interviews Today", so I went in and I was immediately welcomed by Berklee staff. They asked me my name and told me to go into a waiting room. Some of the other applicants were playing guitar. Drummers were practicing with a pad and some people were just sitting down.

It was nearly 9:10 A.M when a woman called my name and asked me if I could have my audition before my scheduled time. She took me upstairs to a practice room and gave me the reading material I was going to be asked to perform during the audition. There room had a few pianos and a keyboard amplifier. Unfortunately there was no guitar amplifier so I couldn't plug in my guitar. I tuned my guitar and practiced the reading material for about ten minutes until the same woman came back and told me it was time to go to the audition room. I took my guitar and pedals, and followed her.

Two Berklee teachers were waiting for me to start the audition—a woman who was a singer and played the piano, and a man with a guitar and a computer. Both teachers were very nice and made me feel very comfortable. They asked me my name, where I was from and what piece I was going to perform. We talked for a little while and then I plugged my three pedals into the Fender Deluxe amplifier provided—everybody usually plays with a Fender amplifier, I gave them a CD with my backing track and plugged my guitar in. Once everything was set up, I started playing my prepared piece, which was an original composition. Though my song was five minutes long, they didn't asked me to stop; they let me play it all the way through.

Right after I was done performing my piece, the professor with the guitar said to me, "Let's go with a blues progression. I am going to play some bass lines and you can lay down some chops". He started playing (without telling me the key) and I improvised. The progression was a twelve bar blues in G. After that, the woman on the piano told me she was going to play a few melodies and that I should sing them back; she must have played five seven-note phrases that I had to immediately sing back. Then I had to do the same thing but on guitar. She played a six or seven note phrase and I had to play it back without pausing to think about it.

Once I was done with the ear training part of my audition, they took out the reading material–which was the same as the one I had in the practice room–and asked me to read it through. The woman on the piano played the chords above the melody. The metronome was probably set at about 140 to 150 bpm. Next, they asked me to play the chords and this time the woman joined me with the melody. The last thing I had to do was the rhythm test. The man clapped a rhythm and I had to clap it back. And that was it; I was done with my audition. The professors were very nice to me; they were constantly complementing me saying, "great man" and "well done". I put my guitar and pedals away, left the audition room and a Berklee staff member told me I had to go one floor up for the Interview.

Once I was on the floor where the interviews were held, a woman checked me in and asked me to wait for a little while. Ten minutes later they called my name and I went into the interview. The person interviewing me was very friendly; he was actually a fifth semester Berklee student. He asked me questions like "Why do you want to study at Berklee?" "What do you want to give to Berklee?" "Tell me about your music training". After fifteen minutes he told me I was done so I stood up, said goodbye to everyone and that was it; all that was left was waiting for their acceptance decision.

On March 4 of 2009 I received an email from Admissions Office telling me that I had been accepted to Berklee College of Music; I was so happy, and I was even happier two weeks later when I got another email from the Scholarship office telling me I had been awarded a scholarship.

Sam Gutman—testimonie
www.myspace.com/samgutman
www.youtube.com/iplayguitar19

First of all, write a few songs and apply for the Writing and Composition Scholarship; it will set you apart and make you stand out from thousands of guitarists. I think that this is the reason that I got in because my actual audition wasn't really exceptional. Seriously, I can't emphasize this enough, apply for that scholarship; it'll help your chances.

There are two parts to the audition: the musical part and the interview. I practiced and practiced and practiced for the musical audition, but never really took the time to think up some good answers to questions such as "What do you feel that you will add to the Berklee community?" and "Why did you choose Berklee?" so as a result I sort of stumbled a bit during the interview. So take the time and really come up with some stuff, so that when they ask you those questions you can be prepared.

Things they asked of me during the audition:

— What is the 6th degree of a D Major scale?

— What is the 5th chord in the key of Eb?

— Improvise in C# Dorian.

— Improvise in Bb Blues.

— Improvise in A Dorian (and while I was improvising he changed the key to G Dorian but didn't tell me, I just had to hear it and follow).

— The guy played chords on the piano and I had to tell him whether the chord was Major 7th, Minor 7th, Dominant 7th, Diminished or Augmented.

The Sight Reading Section

I prepared for this part by working myself through Mel Bay's Guitar Method Grade 1. Before your audition they will give you a page with three short passages written on it. The first passage will be easy, and in C Major, the second piece will be harder, and the third piece will be the hardest. You will have about 15 minutes to practice with this piece of paper before you go into your audition. Use the 15 minutes to learn at least one of the passages because they will ask you to play whichever one best represents your reading ability; I chose the easiest one. They might ask you if you can play one of the harder ones, I told them I couldn't. Also, over the two harder passages on the paper, there will be written accompanying chords, with the chords written over the melody. Learn the chord progressions, I can't stress that enough; it will be all weird chords like m7b5, 7b9, etc. The night

quite easy with just half notes and quarter notes, and the second one involving some 8th notes, ties, and dotted quarter notes. I've only been sight-reading for about 6 months, so I focused on the first two. After 15 minutes of preparation I was brought back out and waited for about 5 minutes to get brought into another room for the audition. While I was waiting I showed one of the students my pedal board that was made out of a briefcase.

I go into the audition room and there are two guys, both very nice; they were cracking jokes and it was a really relaxed cool vibe. We seemed to connect really well, which I was extremely happy about since I knew it was going to give me at least a small advantage. Then I sat down and tuned up. I gave them my CD with the backing track for SRV by Eric Johnson, played through, made a few small mistakes but recovered quite quickly, pretty much playing it solidly. I was happy with my performance. They both seemed pretty happy with my rendition of the song. Then I did some improvisation over a blues progression, which I nailed; it wasn't as good as I wanted it to be, but it wasn't at all bad. I was somewhat disappointed with myself, but I just relaxed and didn't let it get to me.

Then we went on to a call and response thing. The instructor gave me the first note, and then did a small 4 to 5 note phrase, which I had to copy. I did pretty well on this, I stumbled on a few phrases first try, but on the second attempt I got them. I think one phrase messed me up and it took me one more try. So I thought I did pretty well on the call-response portion.

Next we went on to a rhythm thing. They played a rhythm and I had to copy it. We did about a dozen or so different rhythms and got them all right except the last one. But they said that was good, so that was good.

Next up was the reading part. I did the first easy reading part and then I did the second one. First I played the chords, which I did pretty well. The chords where just some m7, m7b5, 7b9, dom7. Then I read the melody of the material; I did get through pretty well.

And that was about it for the audition, we joked around a bit when I was packing up, shook hands, and I went out. All in all, it went well. I connected with them, and think that I did my playing pretty well. Then it was onto the interview.

The interview turned out to be a bit different. I waited in another room for about ten minutes, and then I was called in. The guy was nice; he asked me some basic stuff, first dealing with my musical resume so to speak. I told him how I've been playing for about six years, started taking formal lessons about 8 to 9 months ago. I also made note to mention to him that I never participated in my school band since it's a very big sport school, and the music program is downright lousy. I then just told him about how I was in some bands and stuff, also showing him our bands MySpace. He seemed to enjoy the music.

Then he just asked me the big question "Why Berklee?" To which I basically answered that I wanted to go there for a few reasons:

— The school has an extensive network of connections to good musicians. The faculty members are good well-known teachers.

— I told him I have a real drive and passion for music, and know how much talent is at Berklee ready to be found.

— I told him that would be able to take advantage of what Berklee had to offer, and hopefully be a success later in my life.

— I told him that I knew that Berklee was looking to the future of music more so than some of the other conservatory style schools that I looked at.

— Finally I just noted on the fact that Berklee is in the heart of Boston, which is a good music city.

He then asked me if I had any questions that I felt he should have asked me. I basically told him I couldn't think of any. And that was about it for my interview.

All in all, it went pretty smoothly. I wasn't very nervous, and I was really glad that I connected so well with the audition guys. I just wanted to share my experience with anyone else who is going to audition.

CHAPTER III

PREPARED PIECE

STYLE

Choosing a prepared piece for the audition is probably the most stressful part; having to choose only one piece from your long repertoire always raises the question of "what does the audition team want to hear?" Well, the reality is you can choose whatever you want; there's no limit. Now, the question is, do you really want to choose any song you want? You want to compare your options and choose the song that represents the best of your abilities. Let's take a look at Berklee's Guitar Audition Guidelines from *www.berklee.edu*:

"Berklee embraces and values all music styles so you should prepare a piece that you are comfortable with and displays your strengths as a musician. It should be approximately 3-5 minutes in length, in any style, which demonstrates your instrumental proficiency and your overall musicianship. Do not choose a piece or a style of music you think the audition team wants to hear. Rather, select a piece that puts your "best foot forward" and highlights what you feel represents your best playing. Ultimately, the audition is a discovery process and we want to find out what you do well.

It is recommended to seek the guidance of your private instructor and/or musical mentor when selecting your prepared piece. Here are some examples and additional guidelines that may help when selecting your prepared piece:

A tune from a well-known artist or band (any style)

A standard or jazz tune (which may include blues and rhythm changes) with your own improvisation

A composition from the instrumental/voice repertoire or a movement, sonata, concerto or etude

A transcription of a well-known artist's solo

If composing or songwriting is your primary focus, you may choose to play an original piece that showcases your individual style. However, the original piece should be no longer than three (3) minutes, and you should also prepare a second piece from the above listing (no longer than 3 minutes)."

So after reading these guidelines we can agree that you are able to play anything you want. You could choose any genre like metal, bossa nova, pop, funk, classical music. Whatever style of music you are into, go for it.

Pick the style that shows the best of you, the one you are more comfortable with. Choosing a style or song that you think the audition team will like is not a good idea; they want you to play what best represents you as a musician. You should choose a style in which you are comfortable playing so they can get to know the real you.

STRUCTURE

The structure of your prepared piece is very important. In my opinion, the perfect structure would include a *main melody, jazz harmony, chords, rhythm changes and good technique.*

If you include all of them, your prepared piece will be in good shape for the audition.

Main Melody

This is the most important part of a composition. You should be able to tell a story with sounds; every phrase you play should be connected to each other; what is the point of playing amazing guitar licks if there is no connection between them? Think about a very popular song, like *Somewhere Over the Rainbow*. Now imagine taking out the main melody and leaving nothing but chords. You can improvise over the chord changes and play as many licks as you want, but non of it matters because the essence of *Somewhere Over the Rainbow* is the melody. Without it, the composition does not make sense anymore. And the same thing would happen to your piece if it didn't have a melody. You would be playing different licks over the chord changes, doing some impressive arpeggios and tappings, but none of it would matter because a song with no melody is a song with no feelings. The audition team likes "feelings". Music is a feeling.

Jazz Harmony

Arranging your prepared piece using jazz harmony techniques is generally a good idea. Examples of jazz harmony techniques include Secondary Dominants, Substitute Dominants, Modulation, Modal Interchange, Voice Leading, to name a few. You should either arrange your own composition using jazz harmony techniques or choose an existing song that uses them. I can't stress that enough; using jazz harmony will automatically set you apart from other applicants. By doing so, you will demonstrate your scale knowledge and ability to play over complex jazz progressions. Besides, a song that uses harmony techniques is usually way more interesting than one that doesn't and less cliché. You should at least try to avoid the everyday diatonic progressions (progressions in one key) that most applicants go for.

Another thing to watch is *"knowing what you are playing"*. Let's say you come up with a progression that you like a lot, but you don't really know what it is. You can't come to the audition without truly understanding the harmonic content of your piece; you should be able to analyze the chord progression and the melody relation to the chords. What if the audition team asks you to explain the progression? You should be able to analyze your prepared piece. Besides knowing harmony helps you perform better; it's a fact. Learning harmony could be a tedious process, but it is not hard and once you learn it everything makes sense; you are no longer limited to simple tunes.

Harmony is knowledge; knowledge is confidence; confidence is success. I strongly recommend learning Harmony before choosing or composing your audition piece.

Chords

The guitar is a melodic and harmonic instrument. Unfortunately, most guitar players forget that they can actually play chords and only focus on melodic lines. Your prepared piece should not only be a compilation of melodic lines; you should include a section where you play nothing but chords. It could simply be chords or a melody on top of them. If you decide to play alone (without a backing track or an accompanist), you can still include chords using the technique called Chord Melody in which you play the chords and melody at the same time with one instrument. Most applicants don't choose to play chords in the prepare piece so if you do, you will once again stand out from the rest. For my audition, I played an original composition in rock style that had an epic chord melody introduction.

If you want to learn about Chord Melody there is plenty of material out there. Jody Fisher has a book about chord melody called: "Jody Fisher: Mastering Jazz Guitar - Chord/Melody". And of course you can always go online and learn for free. A good website to learn about chord melody is http://chordmelody.org/ you can also go to any search engine (Google, Yahoo, Alta-Vista, Bing, etc.) and look up "Chord Melody for Guitar". There is also a great DVD by Robert Conti called "Play Pro Chord Melody Today". You can watch a preview on his YouTube channel *www.youtube.com/robertconti.com* and on his official website *www.robertconti.com*

Rhythm Changes

The audition team should never lose focus on your prepared piece. Try varying the rhythm structure of your song; include an A and B section. Avoid jamming over a Vamp (a short chord progression). If you jam over a four-chord progression for three minutes, how's the audition team going to judge you? They will most likely do it based on your melodic lines; you are going to have to work harder on your melodic lines. By varying the rhythm structure your will avoid predictability.

Try to include Odd Meters sections, in 7/8 or 5/4; it will bring a different color to your piece and again, it will make you stand out! Odd meters are on your side; use them.

To find out more about it, look up *"Odd Meters"* in any search engine. You can also try the following websites:

http://www.8notes.com/school/theory/odd_meter.asp
http://www.guitar9.com/columnist74.html
http://en.wikipedia.org/wiki/Time_signature

Good Technique

You should improve your technique as much as you can

before the audition. By doing so, you will avoid predictability. It is very important for you to master all the guitar techniques you plan to use on your prepared piece; this means practicing and practicing a lot every day and paying special attetion to those areas you think you are not doing well. You need to demonstrate that you feel comfortable using most guitar techniques; you can focus on some techniques more than others, but you should be familiar with all of them. And this is not only true for techniques; you should also be able to play arpeggios, some nice bends and some awesome chromatic lines, etc. The main thing to remember is: don't limit yourself and show them all you tricks. It is really important to demonstrate a certain level of maturity in your performance.

Ways to Practice

I would focus on practicing *picking (Alternate, Hybrid, Sweep picking, Economy picking— all kinds of Picking), legato, slide, bend, string skipping, tapping, vibrato and harmonics.*

Try playing arpeggios using some type of picking technique. Use string-skipping or tapping. Play everything as slow as you can and as fast as you can. It is just as important to be able to play at 200bpm as it is at 60bpm. I will repeat this: it is very important to be able to perform your prepared piece at half the normal speed or even slower. If you combine those techniques with improvisation resources, you will stand out from the rest of the applicants.

You can also watch clinics by famous artists like:

— Al Di Meola – REH Master Series

— Eric Johnson – The Fine Art of Guitar

— Frank Gambale – Modes No More Mystery

— Frank Gambale Monster – Licks and Speed Picking

— Joe Pass – Solo Jazz Guitar

— Joe Pass – The Blue Side of Jazz

— John Petrucci – Mystic Dream Exercise (young guitar)

— John Petrucci – Rock Discipline

— Marty Friedman – Extreme Metal Guitar

— Michael Angelo – Speed Kill

— Scott Henderson – Melodic Phrasing

— Paul Gilbert – Intense Rock Complete

— Paul Gilbert – Terrifying Guitar Trip

— Richie Kotzen – Hi-Tech Rock Guitar

— Richie Kotzen – Rock Chops

— Robben Ford - The Art of Blues Solos

— Robben Ford – The Blues and Beyond

— Stanley Jordan – Master Session

— Yngwie Malmsteen – Hot Licks

Those are just a few examples of clinics by famous artists, but there thousands of excellent clinics and videos out there! You can also look up "*Guitar Lessons*" on:

— *www.youtube.com*

— *www.licklibrary.com*

— *www.guitarmasterclass.net*

— *www.guitartricks.com*

— *www.guitarlessons.net*

— *www.guitarlessonworld.com*

You could also learn songs and solos by famous or non-famous artists and apply their techniques to your playing. YouTube and Google are great sites to find either instructional videos or tablatures.

TELLING A STORY

You can use whatever technique you want and change rhythms as much as you want; you can use as many jazz harmony resources as you want, but remember *you are making music*. Every note you play should be a feeling; if there are no feelings in your playing, your performance will be soulless. Be true to yourself; good art comes from your heart, not from your mind. If you compose a melody, always ask yourself first "do I connect to it?". A melody is a mirror of yourself. You should listen to it and connect with whatever it means to you. Musicians tend to learn a melody or lick and play it without wondering if it actually means something to them; they play it because it sounds "cool". A melody is like a tale; it either touches you or it doesn't. You should only focus on music that touches you.

LENGTH

We read in the Berklee Guidelines that the prepared piece should be around 3 to 5 minutes long. The length of the piece doesn't determine if the song is good or not, but if you are planning on playing anything over 3 minutes, you should take some things into consideration.

If you choose a long piece, its harmonic content and structure should be very interesting, otherwise the audition team could most likely ask you to stop playing. For example, if you play an eight-chord piece that lasts five minutes or more, the audition team will ask you to stop playing. You won't make it to 3 minutes because they've heard enough. I know people who were asked to stop playing after 2 minutes of performing their piece and, by analyzing their choice of song I can confirm they all decided to jam over simple progressions that repeated over and over. The following structure would be a bad choice: *verse, chorus, second verse similar to the first verse, second chorus just like the first chorus, simple bridge, verse again and final chorus*. If your harmonic content is not rich, you won't make it to the bridge because the piece will become so predictable that the audition team will think they heard enough.

Play a five-minute song; I played a five-minute song and they never asked me to stop, because my song was rich in harmony, rhythm, structure. I was constantly introducing new things to the audition team—my playing was not predictable.

This is how I structured my prepared piece: I played a one-minute Chord Melody introduction, rich in jazz harmony. Then I turned on my distortion pedal and started playing a two-chord vamp in odd meters for 30 seconds; the rest of the band slowly joined. Next came the first verse, with lots of chords and rhythm changes. The verse was followed by a ten-second pre-chorus, which didn't really lead to a chorus but to the second verse. From the second verse I went to the pre-chorus again but this time leading to the chorus. The chorus was pretty interesting; the progression was somehow similar to the chord melody introduction but of course the melody was different. After the chorus I played a D section followed by section E. These sections were totally different from the rest of the song, but at the same time everything made sense together. After that I played a solo over the verse chord progression. And then I went back to the chorus but slightly changed it and added a new ending. For the last section I adapted the chord melody introduction for a rock context. I changed the progression a little bit but the essence remained.

The main point is that I was always changing, but I never lost the essence of the piece. They never asked me to stop playing; I remember being worried about the length, but they let me play until the end because I kept showing them something new that was related to everything I had previously played.

To summarize: choose a three-minute piece or shorter, or choose a longer piece with an interesting structure and harmonic content. I would go with a longer piece.

INSTRUMENTAL COVERS

I have nothing against Steve Vai, Malmsteen, Satriani or any other well-known artists; in fact I love their music and they have all been huge influences to me. Now here's the thing: everyone loves their music, so 50% of the applicants will be playing their songs. You don't want to choose a piece that other applicants will most likely be playing. Besides, the audition team has already seen other applicants doing this before. Be original; show them something they haven't seen already. Remember: be unique. Avoid this type of songs and especially if they are very well-known. The only time it is acceptable to play a song like this is when you *arrange them or modify them in a unique way*.

CULTURAL PIECES

This is something you really need to consider and especially if you are coming from a foreign country. Berklee is an amazing place where you are constantly surrounded by music from all over the world. Just think about this: you have the option of going for a jazz style song or a unique folk style from your country; what do you think would be better? You are coming to the country where jazz was originated; everyone knows jazz, it's not a new thing. But we can't say the same thing about your unique folk style from your country; you would be performing new music from some other part of the world and believe me, this is what Berklee is about. It is a college open to all styles of music and if your music is innovative, the doors will be open for you.

ARRANGE OTHER ARTIST'S SONG

If you choose to play a tune from a famous artist, please arrange it. Berklee is looking for creative musicians; they don't want an exact copy of a well-known artist. They want to listen to you, discover you, and the only way they can do it is if you show them your musicianship. It is just not a good idea to cover a song just like the original recording. Start by improvising the solo and then try to modify the main melody, the rhythm; try adding some interesting licks in between as well as prolonging sections. I mean, you can cover a song, people usually do that, but don't forget to leave your mark on it. Don't just imitate, work on an arrangement that shows the best of your abilities.

SCORE

It would be great if you could print out the score of your prepared piece, and it would be even better if you did it in Finale or Sibelius. Berklee official notation software is Finale, but Sibelius is accepted as well. Bringing the score is a great idea because not only you'll demonstrate your music notation abilities, but you'll also prove to have a deep understanding of your prepared piece. If you decide to do it, bring at least 3 copies of the score.

BACKING TRACK

If you choose to go with a backing track, I strongly recommend recording it yourself at home. You can use any recording software, generally known as DAW (Digital Audio Workstation), like Pro Tools, Logic, Cubase, Sonar, FL Studio, Nuendo, Ableton Live; you will need an audio interface though. An audio interface will generally bring an in-built preamp, where you can plugin a microphone. If you don't have an audio interface with an in-built preamp, you won't be able to plugin a microphone. Here's a list of software you can get if you are not able to record using an audio interface.

Virtual Amplifier

Use a virtual amplifier is a type of software like: Studio Devil, Guitar Rig, Positive Grid Bias, Eleven Rack, Peavey Revalver, Overloud TH, AmpliTube; you will need a TS/TRS to 1/8 inch adapter and probably an audio driver like ASIO4ALL. If your budget is higher, you could use an AxeFX or a Kemper. For more affordable options you could use a POD by Line 6 or a V-amp by Behringer. I strongly recommend using a Virtual Amplifier if you don't have a good audio interface or good microphones.

Virtual Instruments

To record other instruments like drums, bass, strings, or other instruments, you could go with Virtual Instruments. A virtual instrument is software that emulates a real instrument; in most cases the real instrument has been sampled for the software, so it's literally a real instrument. In other words, you will be able to record real drums with just a few clicks. Some of the most popular drum virtual instruments are: Superior Drummer and Ezdrummer by Toontrack, Addictive Drums by XLN Audio and Battery by Native Instruments. For Bass I recommend: Trillian and Trilogy by Spectrasonics. For orchestra, East West and Vienna are also very good. They both include instruments like violin, violas, flutes, and clarinets, to name a few. There are so many virtual instruments, just do a simple search on the Internet.

If you decide to record your backing track using virtual amplifiers and virtual instruments, the quality will be good. The audition team will give you extra points for this. So, what are you waiting for? Start recording your piece!

So, what should I play?

You have two options:

1. An original composition

2. Your own arrangement of another artist's tune.

Don't cover a song exactly how it's written or recorded.

Second piece

You should also prepare a second piece. If your main piece is an original composition, then your second piece should be a tune by a well-known artist and last no more than 2 minutes. If it's a cover song, make your own arrangement; don't play it just like the recording. Also, try changing the style and orchestration so it's different from the first piece. If you used a backing track in your main piece, then for the second piece play some type of chord melody, just guitar; no backing track. If your main prepared piece is a guitar arrangement with no orchestration or backing track, do the opposite for your second piece and have big orchestration and backing track. I would obviously choose a big orchestration and backing track for the main piece.

Your second piece should be different from your main piece—different style, different jazz harmony techniques, etc. Come up with something different than your main piece. I wasn't asked to perform a second piece, but I know people who were. You should definitely have a second piece ready if your main song is too short. Prepare a second piece.

About the audition

Here's what Berklee has to say about accompaniment for your prepared piece:

"If you require accompaniment for your prepared piece you may bring an accompanist, play-a-long CD or MP3 player. It is not recommended to use the original tracks of artists or bands as play-a-longs. If you are playing to a track, it is preferred that you use standard play-a-long/music-minus-one or karaoke tracks so that you are not playing your part along with the part on the recording. For example, we would prefer a guitar player use a play-a-long track that does not have the lead part on the track rather than playing along with an artist's original recording."

I brought a CD with all the backing tracks I needed for the audition; some applicants brought an accompanist. There was a drummer who brought his brother as an accompanist, who by the way happened to be auditioning that same day. If you are bringing a CD, don't forget to make some copies, just in case one of them doesn't work. Bring the backing tracks in smartphone or an MP3 player if possible; they will have an 1/8-inch cable to plug your device in.

SCHEDULE

Once you have chosen your prepared piece, practice it for *15 minutes, four times a day*. Once you have chosen the second piece, practice it for *15 minutes, twice a day.*

CHAPTER IV

EAR TRAINING

INTRODUCTION

The Ear Training section is a very important part of the audition. Let's take a look at the Berklee's guidelines from *www.berklee.edu*:

"You will be asked to participate in call-and-response exercises. The audition team will play short rhythms and melodies, which you will either sing back or play back on your instrument. You may also be asked to identify intervals and chord qualities. The audition team will also gain a sense of your ability to match pitch during this section of the audition."

So the audition team will play a few melodies and clap some rhythms, which you will have to play back. In this section we will into how to prepare for this part of the audition.

WHERE DO I START?

There are some concepts you need to learn before we start preparing for the Ear Training section of the audition:

Intervals

Intervals are a very important part of ear training. You should learn about intervals and how to use them; learn everything about Intervals.

Scale Structure

Read about the Major scale and its modes. Read about the Harmonic Minor scale and the Melodic Minor scale.

Chord Structure

You need to learn about chord structures. Learn about Triads, their inversions, and also about Four-part chords.

Note Values

If you want to be able to pass any type of rhythm exercise in the audition like rhythm clapping, you need to learn about Note Values. Read about whole notes, half, quarter, eight, sixteenth notes, dotted notes, tied notes; learn everything you can about Note Values.

You can find useful information about these concepts on *www.musictheory.net*, *www.teoria.com* (English and Spanish version), *www.wikipedia.org*, *www.youtube.com* or any search engine like Google, Bing, Yahoo, etc.

I also recommend getting a music theory book such as:

— *Berklee Music Theory: Book 1 - by Paul Schmeling*

— Practical Theory Complete – by Sandy Feldstein

— Music Theory for Guitarists: Everything You Ever Wanted to Know But Were Afraid to Ask – by Tom Kolb - Hal Leonard Edition

— Mel Bay's Easiest Guitar Theory Book

— The Complete Idiot's Guide to Music Theory, 2nd Edition by Michael Miller

— Alfred's Essentials of Music Theory: A complete Self-Study Course for all Musicians – by Andrew Surmani, Karen Farnum Surmani and Morton Manus

Don't continue with this guide until you have learned the four concepts I mentioned. It won't take you more than a day.

CALL & RESPONSE

Call & Response is much more than playing back a melody right after you heard it. There are many things should practice before trying to playback a melody. The secret to succeed in Call & Response is to listen to individual intervals, rather than listening to the melody as one thing. If the audition team plays a five-note phrase, you should immediately be able to recognize the interval between the first and the second note, the second and the third note, the third and the fourth note, and the interval between the fourth and fifth note. In order to successfully do this, you first need learn how to recognize individual intervals; this means learning how to recognize intervals like major third, minor sixth and learning how to do it in any key. The whole point of this is to forget about the tones and focus in the structure of the melody; this is called Relative Ear.

One of the most essential tools in my study of ear training was the software called *Ear Master Pro*. Ear Master Pro helps you recognize every interval. It also helps you practice Rhythm Call & Response by playing rhythms that you have to imitate by either clicking or tapping on the screen.

Ear Master includes many sections that can help you train your ear for the Call & Response part of the audition. I recommend using the following sections of Ear Master Pro to practice Melodic Call & Response:

Interval Comparison

The first step to recognize different types of intervals is to have a sense of interval sizes. If you hear a major second followed by a major sixth, the major sixth interval is obviously bigger. This is the first step and it is very important to practice it until you get a 100% score.

Interval Identification

This part is essential; the software plays two notes and you have to recognize the interval between them. This is exactly what you want to do when the audition team plays a melody; recognize the intervals inside the melody. Pay close attention to backward intervals; the audition team will definitely play melodies composed of backward intervals. The most efficient way to recognize an interval is by relating it to a song you are familiar with. For example, the two notes played at the very beginning of The Godfather movie sound track make a Perfect Fourth. The first two notes in Somewhere Over the Rainbow make a Perfect Octave interval. You should find more songs you know and try to relate them to intervals, that way when you hear an interval the first thing that comes to your mind is "it sounds like this awesome song, it must be a major third". The audition team might also play a specific interval and ask you to identify it by ear, so pay close attention to this exercise.

Chord Identification

In this section EarMaster Pro will play different types of chords and you will have to identify them. This section will be useful for two audition exercises, but for now we will focus on using it melodically instead of harmonically. All chords can be played melodically in the form of an arpeggio; you will have to recognize its quality, meaning major, minor, augmented, diminished, to name a few. This is very helpful because you might run into an arpeggio during the call & response section of the audition. The audition team might also include arpeggios in the melodies they play.

Chord inversions

This section is just like Chord Identification, but it focuses on chord inversions.

Scale Identification

It is very important to be able to identify scales. If the audition team plays a phrase, you should be able to relate each of its notes with a scale degree; if you identify the scale the phrase is in, then you know what notes to use. Besides the audition team might also ask you to identify a scale.

Melody Dictate

This exercise is essential; EarMaster Pro plays melodies and you have to transcribe them. This exercise will introduce you to melodic call & response.

For Rhythm Call & Response, I recommend the following exercises from EarMaster Pro:

Rhythm Reading

You have to read a rhythm from the score using your keyboard or mouse. This exercise helps you get used to basic rhythm patterns.

Rhythm Imitation

This is exactly what you will have to do for your audition; pay close attention to this exercise. A successful way to play a rhythm you just heard is: listen to it, remember it, identify the patterns, repeat it in your head and then clap it; once you have successfully played the rhythm, write it down; this will help you identify similar patterns later.

Rhythm Dictate

This exercise will help you get used to rhythm patterns. Don't try to write down the rhythm at the same time EarMaster Pro plays it; first listen to it, repeat it in your mind, and then write it down. For more advanced exercises including longer rhythms and complex note values I do recommend writing it as you listen to it.

There is plenty of software out there, paid and free; in my opinion, EarMaster Pro is the most complete ear training software I have ever used. I recommend working primarily on EarMaster Pro.

You can buy EarMaster Pro software at *www.earmaster.com*

Auralia by Sibelius is another good ear training software. If you are not satisfied with Ear Master Pro, you can buy Auralia.

GNU Solfege is in my opinion the best free ear training software. If you can't afford paying for software, this is your choice.

If you are unable to work get any ear training software, you can still practice some areas like intervals, chords, scales and rhythm reading. You will have to get a recording device like a mobile phone. Almost any phone now a day includes a recording app. You could also download any type of free recording software like Audacity. Let's say you want to work on intervals; you could record all kinds of intervals you want to practice and then listen to them randomly and try to recognize them. You could do the same thing with chords and scales.

If you can't get an ear training software and you are not able to record the exercises yourself, a private instructor will be your only option. Anyway, with or without EarMaster Pro, you should have a private instructor.

PRACTICE TIME: EAR MASTER PRO

Melodic Call & Response

When you first start using EarMaster, you should work on Interval Comparison for 5 minutes and Interval Identification for 10 minutes. Practice both exercises *3 times a day.*

When you feel you are ready, add Chord Identification for 10 minutes, Chord Inversions for 10 minutes and Scale Identification for 5 minutes. Keep practicing Interval Comparison for 5 minutes and Interval Identification for 10 minutes. Practice all 5 exercises *2 times a day.*

Finally, when you have trained your ear enough to recognize all kind of intervals and main chords, add Melody Dictate for 10 minutes and practice it along with Interval Identification (5 minutes), Chord Identification (10 minutes), Chord Inversions (10 minutes) and Scale Identification (5 minutes). Practice all 5 exercises *2 times a day.* Ear Training is very important, so practice it every day.

Rhythm Call & Response

Start by practicing Rhythm Reading for 10 minutes and Rhythm Imitation for 10 minutes. Practice these exercises *2 times a day.*

Once you feel ready, add Rhythm Dictate for 10 minutes and practice it along with Rhythm Reading and Rhythm Imitation. Do this *2 times a day.*

Though both Melodic and Rhythm exercises are included in the same software, *you should not practice them together*. Take your time and once you are finished with the melodic section, practice other areas for the audition and then go back to the rhythm section of EarMaster Pro.

INSTRUMENT CALL & RESPONSE

The best way to practice Call & Response is with a private instructor; but let's face it, taking private instructions every-day can be a little expensive, so I will recommend some of the software that were essential to me when I was practicing Call & Response:

Sight Singer

This software is actually a melody generator meant to improve your sight-reading, but you can use it to practice call & response because it has a Play function that lets you listen to the melody. When using Sight Singer don't cheat and *don't read the melody from the score*; let the software generate melodies and only listen to them because the idea of this exercise is to *listen and respond*. Sight Singer lets you choose all kinds of melodies, from very easy ones to hard ones. Easier melodies are based on smaller intervals like a second or a third, while harder melodies a re based on bigger intervals like octaves and seventh. You can also choose the phrase length (quantity of notes), the scale and more. The only downside to this software is that it is Windows only. If you decide to use it, I recommend starting with something easy like a three-note melody, in a major scale context. You could slowly increase the difficulty by changing the context to the chromatic scale, or by adding more notes to the melody. You can find Sight Singer software at *www.earpower.com*.

I was doing all right

I actually found out about this software a month before my audition and it was so helpful. I Was Doing All Right will help you with practice melodic Call & Response. There are two sections that I find really useful for the audition; the first section generates melodies and you have to play them back over a backing track provided by the software. In the other section the software will choose some notes, show them to you in the score and then it will randomly change their order and rhythm; you can also choose to not look at the score and recognize everything: the notes, the rhythm and the order.

You can find *I Was Doing All Right* software at: *www.iwasdoingallright.com*

PRACTICE TIME: INSTRUMENT CALL & RESPONSE

Call & Response is a very important section of the audition; practice it every day. You should work with Sight Singer for 10 minutes and I was Doing All Right for 10 minutes *2 times a day*. When you are one-month away from the audition, increase the practice to *3 times a day*.

SOLFEGE AND CALL & RESPONSE

Solfege is a very useful technique that helps you train your ear and improve your pitch and sight-reading. Solfege will help you with Call & Response. Berklee uses Movable Do Solfege, in which every root from a major scale is called Do, every 2nd degree is Re, every 3rd degree as Mi, and so on. Let's say you are in D major scale; in the score you see the notes D, E and F#. Your pitches would be "D, E and F#" but you would say, "Do, Re, Mi". So the tone is the same, but the name is different. It is easy; every scale root is Do. The whole thing about movable-do solfege is to recognize the interval between notes and focus on the structure of a melody instead of trying to figure out each pitch. For example, if someone plays the notes C and E, you should recognize the major third interval instead of trying to figure out what notes you heard, in this case C and E. Or if the audition team plays two notes, E and G, you should try to recognize the interval instead of the actual note, in this case a minor third interval. You should try Movable-do solfege; it will help you train your ears.

But how does solfege connect to call & response? When you practice call & response you want to sing the phrase before playing it, either out loud or in your mind. Once you sing the melody, you have a better understanding of its structure; you can probably recognize all its intervals. Finally, you want to play the melody just like you heard it. This three steps need to be done fast. With time you won't even sing the melody but just play it back instantly. Solfege is the key to call & response; practice it.

If you are just practicing, you can take your time singing a melody; but for your audition day, try to repeat the melody without taking too much time to sing it. I would even suggest to sing it in your mind and as the teacher plays it. Don't take too long to repeat the phrase.

Solfege will also improve your intonation. Sometimes the audition team asks applicants to sing back a melody; this is called the *voice call & response test*. By practicing solfege you are basically getting ready for this part of the audition.

One of the best books about Movable-Do solfege is *Essential Ear Training for Today's Musician by Steve Prosser.*

You can also call the Berklee Bookstore and get class textbooks. You can buy any class textbook you want and they will ship it worldwide at *http://berklee.bncollege.com/*

PRACTICE TIME: SOLFEGE

You should practice solfege at least *30 minutes a day*. If you have time, you can increase the practice to twice a day.

CHORDS

You might be asked to identify chords in your audition. The following tips should guide you to get ready for this section:

Learn the chord structure

If you want to recognize a chord you should first understand its structure. For example, if you want to be able to recognize a maj7 chord by ear, you first have to learn that it is composed by a Root, a Major 3rd, a Perfect 5th and a Major 7th, because no matter how hard you train your ear if you don't know how the chord is built, you won't be able to recognize it. So before trying to practice chord recognition, learn the chord's structure.

Sing the chord

The next step is to sing each note of a chord. Learning the structure of a chord helps you understand the difference between all types of chords. Singing it will helps you hear and feel the difference, and isn't that what it is all about? Chord singing should be done forward and backward; this means from the root to its highest note and from its highest note to the root.

Listen to the chords

As I've said before, the best way to prepare for the audition is with a private instructor. The best way to practice chord identification will obviously be with a private instructor; if you are doing something wrong the instructor will tell you how to improve it. Unfortunately, not all of us can afford a teacher everyday, so you can use EarMaster Pro or other any other ear training software. If you go with EarMaster Pro, you should work on Chord Identification and Chord Inversions. You should do this melodically and harmonically. With or without a private instructor, you should work on EarMaster Pro everyday.

PRACTICE TIME: CHORDS

The first thing you will always do is learning the structure of the chords you will be working on. Practice Chord Singing *10 minutes a day*. You should also use EarMaster Pro and work on Chord Identification for 10 minutes and Chord Inversions for 10 minutes. Do this *once a day*.

ABOUT THE AUDITION

Melodic Call & Response

Both instrument call & response and voice call & response will be the same. The audition team will probably play seven-note melodies to ten-note melodies. My suggestion is to be ready for more; your goal is to be able to respond to twelve-note phrases. The audition team will probably play 5 to 7 melodies; it really depends on how good you are and how much they want to see from you. If you perfectly nail all the melodies, they will probably want you to keep playing until you reach your limit. Be prepared to respond immediately; don't take too long to play the melody back. The melody will include all kinds of intervals, forward and backward, like a minor seventh, a minor third, to name a few.

Rhythm Call & Response

Be prepared to clap long rhythms. For my audition they

ask me to clap a four-measure rhythm! They started with one-measure rhythm and kept increasing the length. The rhythms will probably include tied notes like quarter, eight, triplet and sixteenth notes. You will either have to clap the rhythm or sing it.

Chords

If they ask you to identify chords, they will probably play triads like major, minor, augmented and diminished. They might also play four-part chords like maj7, m7, m7b5, dom7, 7b9, 7#9. They rarely ask you to play major sixth chord, minor ninth chords, but trust me, it is better to be prepared for anything.

Chapter V

Sight Reading

Introduction

Sight-reading is a require section of the audition. Most people are usually worried about this part, and especially guitar players because they are so used to just reading from tablatures. No matter what, the score will always be a more complete way to read music than tablature. You should definitely learn how to read standard notation. Let's take a look at the audition guidelines from *www.berklee.edu*:

"The examples range from basic to complex in order for the audition team to gauge your reading ability. You will have 15 minutes before your audition to warm-up on your instrument and review the reading material before being asked to play the examples in the audition."

It is very important to develop your reading abilities; you should practice it everyday and be ready to sight read any material given to you. So many applicants underestimate the reading section; they think that as long as they are good with the prepared piece and improvisation section, they are in; but that is not true at all. Just imagine you are taking a test and from 10 questions you only know 8 of them. From that test only 10 out 50 applicants will pass; don't you think you would have more chances of passing the test if you answered all the questions? The obvious answer is: yes. The same thing happens with the audition; if you nail all the sections, your chances of getting accepted to Berklee College of Music will be very high.

Getting ready

Some people don't feel comfortable starting off sight-reading a piece. There are a few things you can do first:

Musical Notation Software

These types of software will introduce you to musical notation; you won't be sight-reading but practicing your writing skills. The good thing about it is that you can usually listen to the score. So if you write some non-sense melodies and don't know how it sounds like, you can simply listen to it and start to understand how note values work; you start to understand everything. It is very important to understand musical notation before attempting to sight-read anything. It will be harder for you if you start with sight-reading without knowing anything at all about musical notation. You can use any software like Finale, Sibelius, Guitar Pro, Power Tab.

Clap Rhythms

Melodies are made up of notes and rhythms. Most of the times rhythm is what confuses the reader. You could start off by taking the notes out of a melody and leaving the rhythm, this way you focus on one thing at a time. Let's say you have a melody that combines eight and sixteenth notes and you have never practiced those note value before; it will probably be a challenge for you to read it. But if you did practice these rhythms before, then you won't have any problem reading the melody and you will mostly focus on the notes. You can use EarMaster Pro to practice rhythm clapping using the section called Rhythm Reading. You can also grab your reading material and clap the rhythm of the melody.

Know your scales

You should learn how to play most scale diagrams before trying to sight-read. When you have a lead-sheet, the first thing you want to do is identify the key signature, that way if you are already familiar with the scale you will be using, you only focus on the sight-reading. Your mind makes a relation between a note on the score and a note on the fretboard; when you look at a note on the score, your mind pictures that same note on the fretboard. So if you know the scale diagram before hand, you are half way there. You can find more information about scales and diagrams on any search engine. You could also search for:

— Major Scale Five Positions

— Pentatonic Scale Five Positions

— Minor Scale Five Positions

— Feel free to search for any scale name like "Dorian" and add "Scale Five Positions" right next to it. You will find plenty of information and videos. Some of the scales you can search for are: Major, Dorian, Phrygian, Lydian, Mixolydian, Minor or Aeolian, Locrian, Melodic Minor, Major Pentatonic, Minor Pentatonic, Harmonic Minor.

— You can also find more information about Scales Positions in William Leavitt's Book Series: *A Modern Method for Guitar – Volumes 1, 2 and 3.*

WHAT TO READ

There are six books that I strongly recommend using to practice sight-reading:

A Modern Method for Guitar by William Leavitt

Published by Berklee Press, it is a three-volumes series that will help you develop different areas on guitar. Back in the times when I was preparing for my audition, I only used it for sight-reading purposes. I worked on the reading material, duets, etudes and scale exercises. The book also offers a variety of technique-oriented exercises as well as hundred of chords, but I only focus on sight-reading. The first volume starts off very easy; you get to work on very basic stuff half-note duets, four-measure exercises, etc. You don't really have to work on the three volumes to prepare for the audition, but it is always a better idea to learn more. Whenever you are using this book for sight-reading, do it in position. The first volume focuses more on open-string positions and second position. You need to get used from the beginning to read in position; otherwise it will be harder for you. I strongly recommend beginning your sight-reading studies using A Modern Method for Guitar Volume 1 by William Leavitt.

Melodic Rhythms for Guitar by William Leavitt

Once you are done with volume one of A Modern Method for Guitar, you can start working on this book. Melodic Rhythms for Guitar focuses on specific rhythms and the use of tied notes, rests and syncopations; the reading material is a bit more complex. I strongly recommend this book; the audition material could be a bit similar to the exercises found here. Your rhythm-reading skills will improve a lot with this book.

Reading Studies for Guitar by William Leavitt

This Berklee Press publication is almost like an extension of A Modern Method for Guitar; the sight-reading exercises are very similar but more advanced.

Sight Reading Jazz by Bob Taylor

This is not a beginner's book. The reading material is composed by large intervals like major seventh, major ninth, etc. The rhythms found in this book are not complex at all; the melodies are usually made up of quarter notes or eight notes. I strongly recommend this book because of the intervals.

Eyes and Ears – An Anthology of Melodies for Sight Singing by Benjamin Crowell

This is actually a solfege book, but you can use it for guitar. The material is more classical oriented and it goes from very easy melodies to advanced etudes. As you move forward with this book, the rhythms get more and more complex, while the intervals and choice of notes stay the same.

Advanced Reading Studies for Guitar by William Leavitt

This is your final step for the audition. If you are able to sight-read such high-level material, you are more than done with the reading section of the audition. This book includes complex rhythms and higher scale positions. It also makes use of all key signatures. The audition team usually gives you four sight-reading exercises; two of them are easy and the other two are harder. This book will prepare you for the harder passages.

Read in position; when you start, you should work on lower neck positions and slowly introduce higher positions.

HOW TO READ

Practicing sight-reading everyday is probably the most important advice I can give you; if you don't practice everyday, you won't improve. If you can't find A Modern Method for Guitar, buy any beginner level book. If you don't know how to read at all, you are looking for material that focuses on very basic stuff like half notes and quarter notes. When you are just starting, try setting the metronome to somewhere between 60bpm and 70bpm; you can buy a metronome or use free metronome software online. You should increase the tempo every other week; try to increase it by 10bpm or 5bpm. Don't make sudden tempo changes like 25bpm or more because it will be harder for you and you won't really improve a lot. Sight-reading is an art that takes time to master; don't rush it. If you were to set a goal, 170bpm would be it. You won't be asked to read faster than 150bpm, but if you are comfortable reading at 170bpm, then 150bpm will be very easy. Whenever you are practicing sight-reading. It is very important that you increase the tempo every other week as I previously mentioned. Challenge yourself.

Practice time: Melodic reading

You should start practicing with a Modern Method for Guitar by William Leavitt or any beginner's book you can find and practice for *30 minutes three times a day.*

When you are done with the first book, you can incorporate the second volume of A Modern Method for Guitar, Melodic Rhythms for Guitar and Reading Studies for Guitar. *Practice with each book for 30 minutes.* Don't do one hour and a half of sight-reading because it won't work. Choose one book and read it in the morning; grab the next one in the afternoon and the last book in the evening.

Once you are done with the three books, start working on Sight Reading Jazz by Bob Taylor, Eyes and Ears – An Anthology of Melodies for Sight Singing by Benjamin Crowell and Advanced Reading Studies for Guitar by William Leavitt. The practice should be the same as the second step: *30 minutes for each book.*

You should always go back to the books you already finished. Work with your old books twice a week.

Book alternatives

If you can't find the books I mentioned, you should find alternatives that meet the following criteria:

Level one

Note Values: It should start with very basic stuff like whole notes, half notes and quarter notes; beginners book shouldn't focus that much on eight notes, otherwise the unexperienced reader can find it hard. It could also include tied notes at the end of the book. It may also include whole note rests, half note rests, quarter note rests and occasionally eight note rests.

Key Signature: Entry-level key signatures are C major, F major, Bb major, G major, D major and A major. Eb major could also be included at the end of the book.

Position: Scales should be focused on the first five frets.

Level two

Note Values: Quarter notes, eight notes, triplets and tied notes. You may also find sixteenth notes but not that often. Second level books are focused on eight notes and higher intervals. You may find quarter-note rests and eight-note rests. You may rarely find sixteenth-note rests.

Key signature: All of the previously mentioned scale plus Eb major, Ab major, Db major, E major and B major.

Position: Entry-level scales will now include exercises in higher positions like the eight fret or twelfth fret. New scales exercises will be in middle positions like the eight fret.

Level three

Note Values: All note values could be found in these books. From quarter notes to 32th notes. You will have to work on triplets and complex tied notes. You may also find 8th note rests, 16th note rests and triplet rests. Reading will be harder and harder in this level.

Key signature: All key signatures

Position: All positions; mostly higher positions.

Chords

You will be asked to play the chords above the melody on the reading material. You should learn how to play the following chords all over the neck:

Triads

Major, minor, augmented, diminished, sus2, sus4 and major 6.

Four-part chords

Maj7, m7, m7b5, dom7, 7b9, 7#9, 9, m9, 7#5. Those are the main chords you will need for the audition.

Here is a good way to organize Triads:

C major triad using the 6th, 5th and 4th string

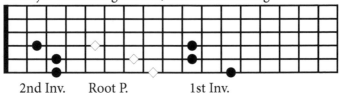

2nd Inv.   Root P.   1st Inv.

C major triad using the 5th, 4th and 3rd string

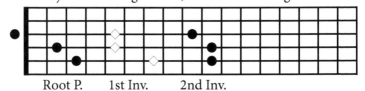

Root P.   1st Inv.   2nd Inv.

C major triad using the 4th, 3rd and 2nd string

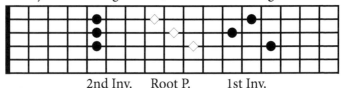

2nd Inv.   Root P.   1st Inv.

C major triad using the 3rd, 2nd and 1st string

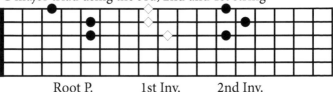

Root P.   1st Inv.   2nd Inv.

Playing four-part chords is a bit different. We are going to use an arranging technique called "Drops". Drop technique is a way to organize chord tones to get a more spread sound and avoid small intervals, which can sound very harsh to the listener. Also, it makes it possible for guitarists to play chords that require huge stretches, like four-part chords. There are different ways to understand Drop technique; I like to see it this way:

For drop II you should send the second note to the end. For example, if you want to play a Cmaj7 that has a C, E, G and B, and you want to apply the drop II technique, you will have to move the E note (which is the second note) to the end. So you will end up having C – G – B – E, which is a Root Position in Drop II:

Cmaj7 using the 5th, 4th, 3rd and 2nd string

Root P.

Let's say you want to play a Cmaj7 in second inversion, but you can't do it because of the stretch; you can't reach the notes. So you use the Drop II technique. To start, a Cmaj7 in second inversion is G – B – C – E, so you send the second note of the position, which is B, to the end and you end up with G – C – E – B, and now you are able to play this chord on guitar.

The following diagrams include all Cmaj7 possible inversions using only Drop II technique:

Cmaj7 using the 6th, 5th, 4th and 3rd string

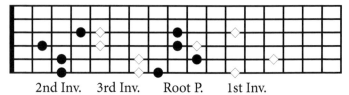

    2nd Inv.   3rd Inv.   Root P.   1st Inv.

Cmaj7 using the 5th, 4th, 3rd and 2nd string

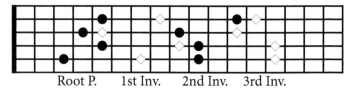

    Root P.   1st Inv.   2nd Inv.   3rd Inv.

Cmaj7 using the 5th, 4th, 3rd and 2nd string

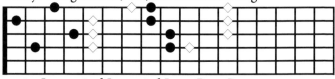

    1st Inv.   2nd Inv.   3rd Inv.   Root P.

How to practice Chords

There are many things you can do to practice chords:

You and a metronome

The easiest way is to come up with some progressions where you include all the chords you want to practice, set up a metronome tempo and start. Your progressions don't have to make any sense at all; you create random progressions with no harmonic meaning. Whatever you do, always use a metronome.

Record some bass lines

You could pretend to be a bass player and record some bass lines over the chord changes. You can literally use any recording device; a mobile phone, a microphone connected to a computer, a camera. You don't have to use a bass, just use your guitar. Don't forget to use a metronome or you won't improve.

Band in a Box

This software lets you insert any chord progression you want and plays it for you. You can choose the style, the tempo, the time signature, key signatures and many other things. Some of the styles it includes are samba, bossa nova, rock, funk, jazz, blues and rap; it is a fun way to practice your chords. The backing tracks usually include drumset, bass, piano, guitar and occasional horns. I strongly recommend practicing your chords on Band in a Box.

The Real Book

There are many versions of The Real Books; there is the original real book, the Latin Real Book, the Blues Real Book, the New Real Book, and more. The real books are a series of compilation of lead sheets for jazz tunes. You could choose two songs per day and work on the chord progressions. This is very similar to what you will be doing in the audition: they will give you a lead sheet with four passages. Each passage will have a melody and a chord progression on top of it. The chord progression will be new to you; just like the random leadsheet from the Real Book you choose to practice everyday.

Sight-reading Chord Progressions by Bob Taylor

This book has easy to advanced chord progressions. The exercises are very interesting; I strongly recommend working on this book.

Always use a metronome or otherwise you won't improve your reading

Your own chord progressions

Here are a few ideas for working on your own chord progressions:

Let's say you want to practice Cmaj7 and its inversion. You open Band in a Box and insert a Cmaj7 chord and repeat it for as many times as you want. You will play a Root position on the first measure, a first inversion on the second measure, a second inversion on the third measure, a third inversion on the fourth measure and then go back. You could also skip inversions and go from the root position to the second inversion, back to the first inversion and so on.

Another thing you can do is, insert random chords; for example, you can play a Cmaj7 on the first measure, an Ebmaj7 on the second measure, an Abmaj7 on the third one and a Gbmaj7 on the fourth measure. You can play first inversions on all the chords, or you can play root position on the first chord, first inversion for the second chord and so on. You can also choose an inversion for the Cmaj7 chord and then decide of the inversions based on how close they are to the Cmaj7. These are just a few ideas; feel free to explore and come up with more.

For a more advanced practice you can work on progressions that have different types of chords. You can add a Cmaj7 in the first and second measure, a Dm7 in the third measure and G7 in the fourth measure. You can come up with as many combinations as you want, use any key signature you want and any chord you feel like practicing. Also, if you are having trouble with a specific section of a tune, you can add it to band in a box and practice it using all the exercises I mentioned above.

PRACTICE TIME: CHORDS

The next schedule will be very useful

The first thing you want to do is learn different types of chords. You can set a metronome or open band in a box, choose the chord you want to work on and practice it. Don't work on more than one chord at a time; take you time and learn each chord very well. You always want to be as organized as possible otherwise you don't really learn everything. You could choose four types of chords (e.g. maj7, m7, m7b5 and dom7) and divide them in 2 groups and spend 15 minutes on each chord. So you can practice the first two chords for 15 minutes each, go on to another exercises like improvisation and later go back and practice the two remaining chords for 15 minutes each. To summarize, you have to practice chords for *30 minutes twice a day*. You can change chords every three days. You can also go back to chords you already practiced and mixed them up with new chords and practice all of them together.

Once you feel comfortable playing different types of chords, you can start mixing up more than one chord in a progression. You can set up a metronome or Band in a Box and come up with as many chord combinations as you want; try not to use more than four chords in one progression. You could practice four chords like a maj7, a m7, a m7b5 and dom7. I recommend practicing this area for *30 minutes twice a day*. Be creative and add some variety to your work. Don't just practice the same chords and progressions every day; change the chord type, change the order, change the inversion. For new chords, always practice them separately; the same applies to chords you are having trouble with. If you decide to include new chords, *practice them separately, following directions from step one, for 15 minutes a day and a minimum of four times a week*. Once you feel comfortable with the new chords, you can incorporate them to the new routine.

The third thing you can do is work on long progressions. You can work on tunes from the Real Book or any other book I mentioned before. You will also continue to practice any new chord, like mentioned in the first two steps. Practice long progressions for *30 minutes twice a day*. When using the Real Books, set up a metronome and play the chords above the melody. I recommend using the first 20 minutes to work a lot on one tune you choose and the last 10 minutes to simply sight-read random tunes from the real book. Try to use as many inversions and neck positions as possible. For the other 30 minutes, you should choose another book and work on it. You can do it just like the Real Books.

ABOUT THE AUDITION

Melodic Sight Reading

The sight-reading section of the audition will consist on three to four short melodies. The melodies will probably be eight measures long:

The first melody will be very easy; it will probably be in C major, using very basic note values like quarter notes, half notes and occasional eight notes. It might also be written for an open string position. No matter what, don't use an open string position; always do your best. Open string position is seen as a beginner's choice. The only case you could use an open string position is if the melody includes arpeggios.

The second melody will use eight notes, tied notes, quarter notes and half notes; it will probably be in F major, Bb major, G major or D major. It will probably be written for a second position scale, which means you won't be reading higher than the fifth fret.

The third melody will be on the harder side; it will have eight notes, tied notes and occasional sixteenth notes. The actual difficulty of this passage will be the neck position; the melody will be written for a higher neck position like the ninth fret or the twelfth fret. The key signature will probably be Eb major, D major, A major or Ab major.

The last melody will be the hardest one. It will have triplets, eight notes, tied notes and sixteenth notes. There will be less or non quarter notes and half notes. The intervals will be as big as a major seventh. The key signature will probably be Ab major, E major, Db major or B major. On rare cases, the key signature could be Gb major or F# major. The melody will be written for a higher neck position like the twelfth fret or even higher.

The tempo will be somewhere around *140bpm to 150bpm*. Sometimes they don't even let you know the tempo and just turn the metronome on; but sometimes they do ask you at what tempo you want to read the melodies.

Chord Sight Reading

You will be asked to read the chords above the melody. The four melodies will include chords. The passages should look something like this:

    All melodies will include jazz chords. I can say that the last two passages will have more chords than the first two; this means that instead of one or two chords per measure there will be two, three or four chords per measure. All the chords will most likely be four-part chords, and mostly seventh chords; this means maj7, m7, m7b5, dom7, 7#5, 7b9, m9, etc. You will have to follow the changes with a metronome. Whatever you do, don't stop; if you make a mistake, keep on going and try to catch up. They won't ask you to read the chords above all 4 melodies; they will probably choose one or two passages and ask you to perform the chords while they play the melody. In my audition they only asked me to play the chords from the melody I had previously read.

CHAPTER VI

IMPROVISATION

INTRODUCTION

The Improvisation section is one of the most important parts of the audition process. In this section you will demonstrate your technique, your knowledge of jazz harmony, your creativity and versatility; you will show them what makes your playing so special. In this section I am going to talk about all the things you can do to develop your improvisation skills. Let's take a look at the audition guidelines from *www.berklee.edu*:

"We would like to hear you improvise over a short progression to gauge where you are in your instrumental development. Your prepared piece may include improvisation, but it is not required.

Blues: You should be prepared to play over a standard I-IV-V blues progression"

It's easy; you will have to *improvise a solo* over any chord progression they want.

YOUR PREPARED PIECE AND IMPROVISATION SECTION

Your choice of prepared piece is related to the improvisation section. Let's say you choose to play a Blues for your prepared piece; I guarantee you that the audition team won't ask you to improvise over a blues progression. Their choice of style and chord progression for the improvisation section will probably be the opposite of your prepared piece. Why? Because they want to see how versatile you are. Another case could be that you choose a jazz tune for your main piece, and you would most likely improvise a solo; chances are that they won't ask you to solo to a jazz progression in the Improvisation section. Don't get me wrong though; this doesn't mean that if your prepared piece is a Blues tune you won't have to practice blues in the improvisation section. *Always practice everything in case things are different on your audition.*

IMPROVISATION: WHERE TO START

There are some concepts you should understand before you start practicing for the improvisation section of the audition.

Jazz Harmony

Before even trying to read about improvisation, I would learn Jazz Harmony. Jazz Harmony will help you understand the relationship between chords and scales; you will learn to use the right scale with the right chord. Learning jazz harmony is very important; it literally frees your mind. Even if you are the type of musician who doesn't like the concept of "right and wrong notes", harmony will still be useful; because there is no better way to free yourself from the ordinary than knowing and experiencing the ordinary. You will never be able to free your mind if you don't understand the concepts that suppress it. Playing by ear will get to a point where you can't really improve anymore; you will think that you ran out of ideas, but the truth is that you can't translate your feelings into musical notes, because you don't understand them. Harmony will help you understand yourself as a musician. The following harmony books are very interesting:

— *Berklee Music Theory Book 2: Fundamentals of Harmony by Paul Schmeling*

— Jazz Harmony by Andy Jaffe

— Mel Bays Complete Book of Harmony Theory and Voicing

— Harmony and Theory by Carl Schroeder and Keith Wyatt

— Concepts of Jazz, for all musicians by Bill Palmer

If you are interested in a harmony book that I have not mentioned, read it; there are great harmony books out there. You may find more books from publishers like Berklee Press, Aebersold, Mel Bay, Hal Leonard and Advance Music.

Scales

Knowing your scales all over the neck is the first step to improvisation. Scales and harmony study should be connected to each other; the scales you should practice are those you learn in your harmony books. There is no point on learning a scale you don't really know how to use; that's why you should first understand its function in a progression and then play it on guitar.

I recommend using backing tracks to practice your scales. You could use any of the methods I previously mentioned: you and a metronome, a recorded bass lines or *Band in a Box*. You should organize your scales in five or seven positions.

At first you could choose a scale, like the major scale, and play a root position in different keys like C, Bb, Ab and Eb. If we follow the previous example, you would play a C major scale in root position, a Bb major scale in root position, an Ab major scale in root position and an Eb major scale in root position. This is just an example; you could use any key you want and organize them however you want.

The only down part to the previous example is that the chord changes will sound a bit weird, but it will still get the job done. If you want the progressions to be a little bit smother, you could choose a scale, like the Lydian Scale, and play the characteristic chord (maj7#11) in different keys. Your progression might look something like this:

Cmaj7#11 – Eb maj7#11 – Abmaj7#11 – Dbmaj7#11 - Amaj7#11

The progression you write down doesn't have to make sense at all; the whole purpose of this is to practice scales. In the example above, you would play the C Lydian scale, the Eb Lydian scale, the Ab Lydian scale, the Db Lydian scale and the A Lydian scale. When you are working on scales, you need to be your own instructor. For example, if you feel like you are having trouble with a scale position, you can create come up with exercises where you use the scale position; the exercises can be like the ones I mention above.

Here is a list of short progression, usually called Vamps, that will give you the sound of a particular scale:

C Ionian or Major Scale: *C - F*
C Dorian: *Cm – Eb* or *Cm – Dm*
C Phrygian: *Cm – Db* or *Cm – Fm*
C Lydian: *C – D* or Cmaj7#11 by itself.
C Mixolydian: *C – Bb – Am*
C Aeolian or Minor Scale: *Cm – Ab – Bb*
C Locrian: *Cm7b5*
C Harmonic Minor: *Cm – Ab – G*
C Dorian #4: *Cm7 – D7*
C Mixolydian b9/b13: *C – Db*
C Melodic Minor: *Cm6 – Dm6*
C Lydian b7: *C7 – Daug/C*

You could also come up with a chord progression and

modulate it. For example, if you are playing the C major scale over Dm – G7 – Cmaj7, you can modulate it a whole step down every time, like this:

C Major scale	Bb Major scale	Ab Major Scale
Dm7–G7–Cmaj7	**Cm7–F7–Bbmaj7**	**Bbm7–Eb7–Abmaj7**

This is just an example; you could do the same thing but using thirds, fourths or any interval you want. You don't need an interval structure; you can modulate randomly.

One thing I like to do with tunes I've never practiced before is follow the chord changes playing only scale patterns up and down. There are many things you can do to practice scales; don't limit yourself and be creative.

AND, HOW DO I IMPROVISE?

Knowing your scales is only the beginning of improvisation. Improvisation is little bit like speaking; you can memorize the entire alphabet or remember how to pronounce certain words, but if you can't really come up with a sentence, there is no point. With improvisation you can memorize every possible scale, but if you don't really know how to use those scales to come up with a really nice melody, there is no point. Improvisation is all about combining notes from or outside of a scale to create a melody that represents the feeling you want to share with the listener. Improvisation frees your mind.

To me, the improvisation study should be divided in three sections:

— *The Understanding Section*

— *The Listening Section*

— *The Practicing Section*

THE UNDERSTANDING SECTION

In this section you will only focus on understanding the art of improvisation. You won't be playing with your instrument, you will either be reading from a book or listening to your teacher; you will only pick up your guitar to have a better understanding of the concepts, not to practice them. I recommend finding a good private instructor who can teach you a lot about improvisation. I lso recommend learning from books. The following books are essential for the Understanding section:

How To Improvise: An Approach To Practicing Improvisation by Hal Crook

— The Art of Improvisation by Bob Taylor

— The Guitarist's Guide to Composing and Improvising by Jon Damian (Berklee Press Book)

— Jazz Improvisation for Guitar: A Melodic Approach by Garrison Fewell (Berklee Press Book)

— Playing the Changes: Guitar by Mitch Seidman and Paul Del Nero (Berklee Press Book)

— Joe Pass Guitar Style by Joe Pass and Bill Thrasher

— A Chromatic Approach To Jazz Harmony And Melody by David Liebman

There are so many improvisation books in the market and most of them are very good; I can only recommend the books I have used, but this doesn't mean that the books I haven't mentioned are not good; in fact, in you interested in a book I haven't mentioned, go for it. Improvisation is not like jazz harmony; the concepts will vary a lot depending on the author. You may find more books from publishers like *Berklee Press*, Aebersold, Mel Bay, Advance Music and Hal Leonard.

The best way to learn improvisation is with a private instructor and a book; your teacher should be your guide, but at the same time you should also try to learn by your own. Don't completely rely on a private instructor; he might be a great instructor and teach you most of the concepts but it is always a good idea to also learn on your own.

THE LISTENING SECTION

In this section you will listen to artists you like and transcribe their songs; this will help you expand your music vocabulary and come up with better melodies. Having musical influences is very important for every musician. It will shape your sound and playing; you will learn from listening to other artists and you will apply everything you learned to your work. It is not really copying; it is inspiration. Whenever you listen to other artists, transcribe their music and analyze; include the melodies you learned in your playing just like you heard them. Alter the melodies and combine them with your own lines. Come up with new melodies inspired by the ones you transcribed. Expand your music library; listen to as many artists as you can. Learn from your friends, learn from your band mates; share your knowledge as much as you can.

THE PRACTICING SECTION

In this section you will finally be able to improvise using your guitar; you will apply everything you've learned (in the Understanding section and Listening section) to your playing. In the audition you will be asked to improvise over a chord progression. Improvisation is not about playing the right scale; in fact you don't even have to play the "right notes" over a chord. To be honest with you, the audition team won't care if you play the right scale or not; they will want to listen to your improvisation ideas, to the melodies you play; they will want to see a certain level of maturity in your improvisation, which doesn't come from knowing how to play the right scale over a chord. Maturity comes from knowing how to tell a story using sounds; maturity comes from knowing how to create interesting melodies. This is why the Practicing section is so important, because you will apply all these concepts to your playing; you will use scales to create beautiful melodies.

You should follow the next steps to practice:

When you are just starting improvising, work on short chord progressions; don't modulate and use one key signature per chord progression. Your main focus is applying the improvisation techniques you learned to your playing; this is why at first you shouldn't work on more advanced progressions which require you to play different scales. You want to focus on one thing at a time for now; you will have plenty of time later to go crazy with more advanced progressions. Remember, work on short progressions that require one scale. Also, try to apply no more than two improvisation concepts at a time.

As you feel more comfortable with some of the improvisation concepts, you should practice them over a more advanced progression, which requires more than one scale. It is very important that you choose a scale diagram to work on; you want to be as organized as possible; using different scale diagrams will only confuse you. For example, you can work on five different position of the D Dorian scale, but don't use them all in one progression. Take your time and practice them separately. When you feel more comfortable, you can combine them. But remember, your main focus is always, the improvisation techniques.

Finally, when you feel very comfortable improvising using different scales, you should work on real tunes, like the Real Book.

Real Books are usually full of tunes (mostly jazz). I recommend analyzing the chord progression of any tune you want to work on, either by yourself or with the help of an instructor. Also, there are plenty of websites where you can find the analysis for many of the tunes from the Real Book. Once again, analyze the tune you will be working on; know before hand what scales you are supposed to use over each chord. Analyze your options.

CHORDS

It would be a great idea to add chords to your improvisation. Adding chords will most definitely change the color and vibe of a tune, which can be a good thing, or a bad thing. I personally think they are more interested in your melodic improvisation, but adding a passage using chord-melodies, where you play the melody and chord at the same time, would be awesome. Don't do it for more than 4 measures though. This is not the same as using a chord to approach a note or as a final tone; you can definitely use chords in your improvisation. I'm talking about an evident use of chords, where every note you play is accompany by a chord.

Practice time: Improvisation

You can follow this schedule:

Spend *30 minutes a day* working on the Understanding Section, reading a Book. Take notes of everything you learn so you can later practice it on your guitar.

Spend *30 minutes a day* listening to music that inspires you. Listen to it, transcribe any solo, analyze the solo in relation to the harmony and try to play it. Work on the same song for more than one day until you have totally mastered it.

Spend *20 minutes, twice a day*, working on the Practicing Section. Choose a progression that feels right to you and work on it. Make a list of all the concepts you have learned so far in the Understanding and Listening section and practice them using your guitar. Practice each concept until it feels natural using it.

Spend *20 minutes a day* practicing all the concepts you already mastered. You should keep working on every improvisation technique you have already mastered.

About the audition

Once you have performed your prepared piece, the audition team will probably ask you to improvise; sometimes they ask you to do it after the sight-reading section. They might say something like "Ok let's go with a Blues", "Let's jam for a little while". They won't tell you what scales you can use to improvise, you will have to listen to the chord progression and decide. Sometimes they might not even tell you what chord progression they are going to play. As I mentioned before, if you played a jazz tune or a blues tune for your prepared piece and you didn't improvise a solo, they might ask you to improvise over the changes. *Be aware of modulation and chord changes.* They asked me to improvise over a blues progression and didn't tell me the key; I had to figure it out. They also added a random Jazz Blues turn around without letting me know; I had to follow. Another thing to be aware of is modulation. If you are improvising over a G Dorian vamp (short progression), they could modulate to another key like a Bb Dorian, keeping the same vamp structure. My advice for you is: Keep playing, no matter what happens; don't stop playing. Don't ask them anything about the improvisation; just start playing. Only ask them something if you really don't know what they are talking about.

Chapter VII

The Interview

You will also have to participate in a fifteen-minute interview with a Berklee Admission representative, which will happen on the same day as your audition and in the same building. During the interview you will have to talk about yourself, sharing information like musical background, goals, why you have chosen Berklee and more. The Interview is not a process that you can fail or succeed; it is an opportunity where you can introduce yourself to Berklee, so don't be nervous; relax and be yourself. Here are some of the usual questions applicants get during the interview:

— Why do you want to study at Berklee College of Music?

— What will you bring to the Berklee community?

— How long have you been playing your principal instrument for?

— Do you play any other instruments?

— Have you ever won any type of music contest?

— Tell us a little bit more about your past achievements as a musician.

— What do you expect Berklee to give you?

— What do you want to major at?

— They may also refer to your online application for more information.

Upload your music to Soundcloud, Youtube or any online service. Berklee is no longer accepting CDs or DVDs so do not waste your time and energy bringing the CD of your band to the Interview. If you want to share your music, you can show them a website (personal website, Myspace, SoundCloud, Youtube, etc) and they will add it to your application and listen to it later.

Though the interview process is really just about being yourself, there are many things you should prepare before hand:

Write down the answers to every possible question, it will help you be your best self at the audition. Get to know yourself; the best answers come from inside.

Share your answers. Once you have a few possible questions & answers written down, share them with your friends, instructors, family and whomever you want. This will help you nail the interview.

Chapter VIII

Preparation &Tips

Psychologically Ready

Being psychologically ready for the audition is one of the most important things. It has happened to all of us at least once; you spent so much time rehearsing for a gig, just to go on stage and let the nerves get the best of you. My experience has shown me that most of the time there is something we are doing wrong during our training, especially if this keeps happening.

The secret to give a perfect audition is to be 100% confident about your playing and knowledge. There are many things you can do to increase your confidence:

Be a strong person

Don't be afraid about what the audition team or others might think about your prepared piece or playing. Be strong; be your best self. Know that you are the incredible. The moment you start doubting about your musical strengths, you fail. Fall in love with your music; be obsessed with the way you play. You are the man.

Practice as much as you can before the audition

You can't be ready for the audition in one month; take your time and practice as much as you can. I read about people who had their audition in two weeks and they still hadn't chosen a prepared piece! Make sure you don't do that. You need to take your time with this; you need to carefully read though the audition requirements and practice a lot. I recommend every musician who is planning to audition for Berklee to spend at least one full year getting ready for the audition. If you are already very familiar with most of the things I mentioned in this book, spend at least two months focusing only on the audition. Don't forget that it takes time to your muscles to remember what you play; it's not a one-day thing. When the audition day comes, you need to be completely sure about your skills and material, and you will only be able to achieve this if you practice a lot.

Play live as much as you can

Live performances will make you feel more comfortable when playing in front of strangers; you should perform your prepared piece, improvise over a backing track and participate in Call & Response jams with other musicians. These days you don't even need a band to play in venues; you record a backing track at home or buy a looper pedal and you are done. You can use a guitar amp or an amp simulator like POD by Line 6, AxeFX and V-amp by Behringer. If possible, play in front of people you don't know at all; playing for your friends and family is a good place to start, but in the long way you want to play for strangers; it's just a complete different thing.

You nailed the audition

You have to be positive! The mind is very powerful. Every time you think or talk about the audition, be positive and imagine being successful. If you say, "Oh my god, I really hope I don't make any mistake", then you will probably make a mistake. You should only focus on success; failure should never be an option. Remember, the audition team doesn't want you to fail; they actually want to see the best of you. You should be excited, happy and positive all the time no matter what. I mean, you are having an audition for Berklee College of Music, which is the best music college in the world, how awesome is that? And you are actually audition to be a part of this unique and inspiring place. Just think about all the good things that will happen once you get accepted to Berklee; think about how much you will grow as a musician, think about all the people you will meet. Don't forget, be positive and you will succeed.

Tips for the day of your audition

Eat healthy before your audition

You don't want to risk feeling bad during your audition. You should really eat healthy food two days before the audition; this means no burgers or fried food.

Sleep Early

The last thing you want is to feel tired during your audition. Go to sleep early. Get at least eight hours of good sleep.

Set at least two alarms to wake up on time

If your audition is schedule in the morning, set an alarm to at least three hours before the audition. My audition was schedule for 10A.M, so I woke up at 7 with the alarm and also had my parents call me in case I didn't hear the alarm.

Be prepared audition before your scheduled time

This is very common, especially in Boston where many applicants can't make it on time or simply decide to not take the audition and forget to cancel it. You should be prepared to audition before your scheduled time. I had my audition before the schedule time.

Get your gear ready before going into the practice room

If you have a pedal board or any type of pedal; if you need to tune up your guitar, do it before going into the practice room. When you get into the building where you will have your audition, you are taken to a waiting room with other applicants, parents and Berklee staff. You want to use that time to get your gear ready.

Warm up in the waiting room

Take your guitar our and warm up; it is the perfect time to jam a little bit. Do not warm up in the practice room; use it to practice the sight-reading material.

Make some friends

Talking to other before the audition will help you be more relaxed. And, your networking starts that day.

Be well dressed

I'm not saying you have to wear a suite and tie, but dress up like if you were going to a nice nightclub.

About the Author

Matias Rengel is a graduate of Berklee College of Music, where he majored in Music Production and Engineering. He has been playing guitar since 1999.

At Berklee, he studied with some of the best teachers around the world, including Tim Miller, Norman Zocher, Jim Kelly, David Fiuczynski and Andrew Maness. He was also part of the Berklee Singers Showcase which features some of the most talented musicians in school. His recordings and productions were among the best, having one of them selected for the annual MP&E showcase.

As an entrepreneur, Matias co-founded SoundTwirl, the most complete and versatil jamming app on the market. He also co-founded ExpressDrummer.com - a collection of high quality Drum Samples recorded and mixed by him. He has also published "299 Insane Guitar Licks", a guitar instructional book.

Matias currently resides in Boston, MA, where he plays with People The Kangaroo, an electronic indie band. He is also working on his first solo album as an EDM producer, which will be released in 2015.